# The Starry Sky

First published 1994

1 3 5 7 9 10 8 6 4 2

Copyright © Aladdin Books Limited 1994
An Aladdin Book
Designed and produced by
Aladdin Books Limited
28 Percy Street
London W1P 9FF

*Design:* David West Children's Book Design

*First published in the United Kingdom in 1994 by*
Riverswift, Random House, 20 Vauxhall Bridge Road, London SW1V 2SA

*Illustrations by* Paul Doherty
*Additional illustrations by* Mike Lacey and Ian Thompson
*Photocredits:* Pages 16 and 72: Science Photo Library; page 28: Melies
(Courtesy Kobal Collection); page 32: Frank Spooner Pictures; pages 36 and
37: Roger Vlitos.

Random House Australia (Pty) Limited, 20 Alfred Street, Milsons Point, Sydney,
New South Wales 2061, Australia

Random House New Zealand Limited, 18 Poland Road, Glenfield, Auckland
10, New Zealand

Random House South Africa (Pty) Limited, PO Box 337, Bergvlei, South Africa

Random House UK Limited Reg. No. 954009

A CIP catalogue record of this book is available from the British Library

ISBN 1 898304 03 3

Printed in Belgium

*My grateful thanks are due to Paul Doherty for his splendid
pictures, and to Lynn Lockett for all her help and encouragement.*
P.M.

# Patrick Moore

# The
# Starry
# Sky

Riverswift
London

# Contents

# Foreword

Have you ever looked up into the sky and started to think about what you can see there? The Sun, the Moon and the stars shine down, but not everyone takes the trouble to find out just what they are. I was six years old when I began to take an interest in them. In this book I have done my best to help you in making a start, and I hope that you will be interested enough to go on and make a real hobby out of astronomy. If you do I am sure that you will enjoy it, because there is so much to see, and there is always something new to find out. I wish you the best of luck!

*Patrick Moore*

The Sun and the Moon as seen from Earth.

# The Sun and its family

All our light comes from the Sun. It is so bright that you must never look straight at it or you will hurt your eyes badly. The Sun is much bigger than the Earth, and it is a very long way away. The Earth moves round the Sun, taking one year to make the full journey. There are

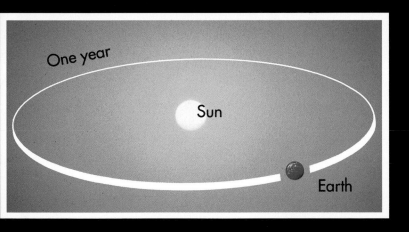

eight other bodies of the same kind, which we call planets. Some of the planets have moons; we have one, our own Moon, which shines because it is being lit up by the Sun. As well as the planets and their moons, there are many bodies in the Sun's family, and I will talk about all of these in this book.

# The Earth and its air

The Earth is shaped like a ball. We live on its surface, and we do not fly off because of a force called gravity, which holds us all down. If you throw a stone upward, it will soon fall down again, because the Earth's gravity will not let it go. The air around us is made up of gas. If you swish your hand, you can feel the air being pushed out of the way. But the air does not spread upward forever. The higher you go, the less air there will be. On the tops of some mountains, the air is so thin that you could not breathe it. Out in space there is no air at all.

Mountaineers need to wear oxygen masks when very high up.

When you are travelling in space, you seem to have no weight at all.

Sometimes you can see the Moon in the daytime sky.

# The Sun and Moon in the sky

When it is daytime, and there are no clouds, you can see the Sun. At night you can often see the Moon. But do you know what the Sun and the Moon are really like? The Sun is much the bigger of the two, but the Moon is much closer to us. You already know that the Earth moves round the Sun. The Moon moves round the Earth, taking just over 27 days to do so.

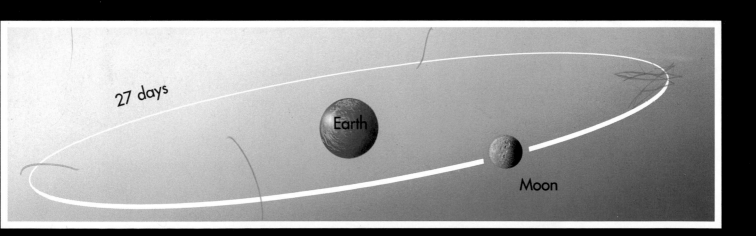

27 days

Earth

Moon

The Moon has no light of its own, and shines only because it is

# Looking at the Sun and Moon

The Sun is very hot. If you hold out your hand to the Sun, you will feel the heat. The Sun is also very bright. You must never look straight at the Sun. Astronomers use solar telescopes which reflect an image of the Sun. The Moon sends us almost no heat. You can look straight at the Moon for as long as you like and you will not hurt your eyes.

Here an astronomer is measuring the sizes and positions of sunspots, using a very large telescope in America. Even then, the astronomer must wear dark glasses to make sure that he does not hurt his eyes.

Heat from the Sun is so strong that it can quickly burn your skin.

# How the Sun moves

The Earth turns round once in every 24 hours, so that to us it seems that the sky moves round from east to west – taking the Sun, the Moon and the stars with it. This is why the Sun seems to rise in the east and set in the west every day.

The Sun is higher in the sky in summer than in winter, which is why the days in summer are so warm. When the Sun is low down in the sky, its light comes to us through a thicker part of the Earth's air. This makes the Sun look orange or red. Even then you must never look straight at it. Do not forget this; you must not hurt your eyes.

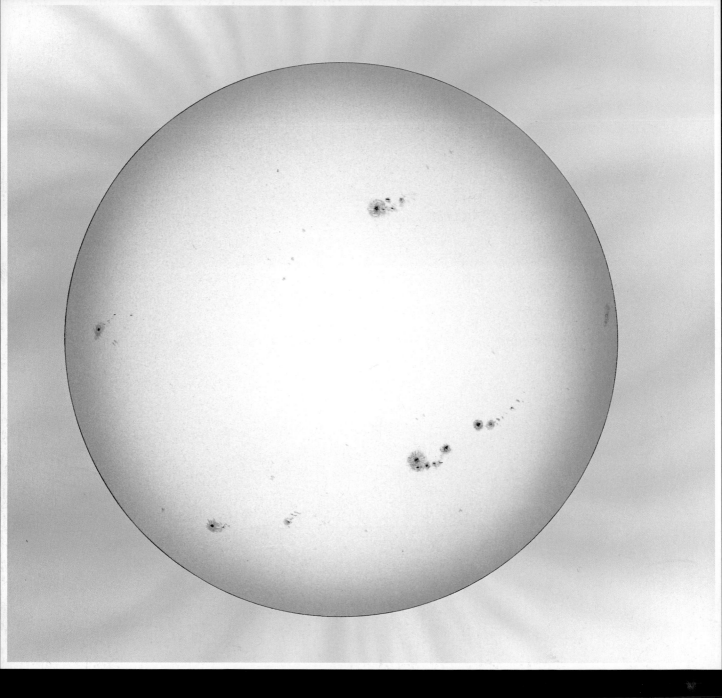

Dark 'sunspots' are cooler patches in the Sun's hot gas.

# Spots on the Sun

The Sun is very much bigger than the Earth. It is not solid, but is made up of gas, so you could not go there even if it were not so hot! Like the Earth, it is spinning round, but it takes nearly four weeks to make one full turn instead of only 24 hours. Sometimes there are dark patches on the Sun. These patches are called sunspots. They look black because they are not so hot as the gas around them. They do not last for more than a few days or a few weeks, and at times there may be no sunspots at all.

21

# How the Sun shines

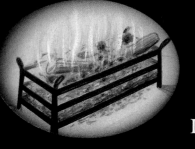

The Sun is not burning in the same way as a fire. It is very much hotter than any of the fires we have in our houses. Inside the Sun, one kind of gas is changing into a different kind of gas, and this process is what makes the Sun shine. The Sun is very old – much older than the Earth – and it hardly changes at all. If it became even a little hotter or a little cooler, the Earth would become either too warm or too cold for us to live here.

The Sun's heat is much weaker at the Earth's Poles, so that the climate there is cold.

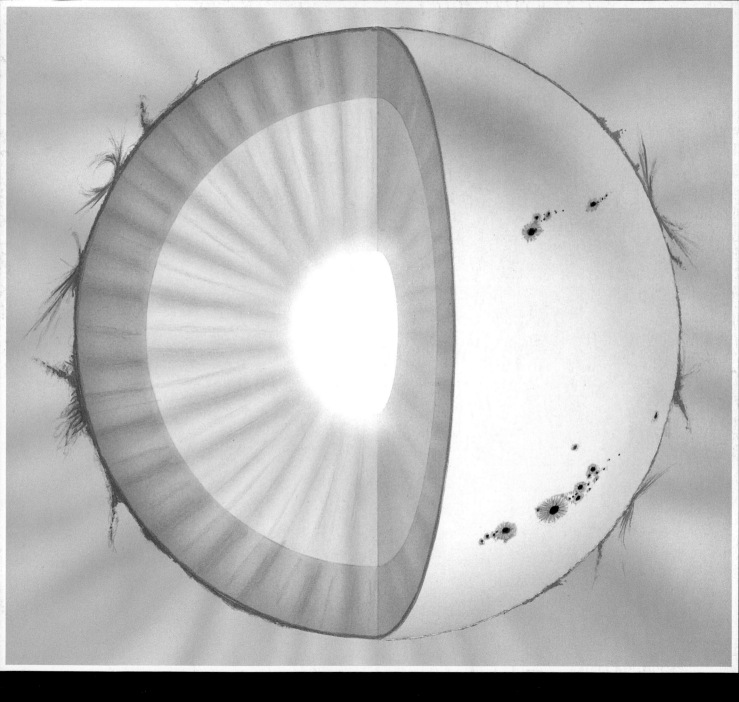

The Sun is much hotter inside than it is at its surface.

# *Hide and seek*

Sometimes the Sun, the Moon and the

Earth move into a straight line, with the

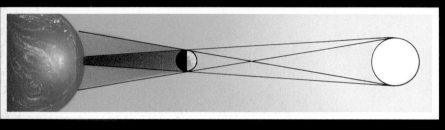

Moon in the middle. When this happens,

the Moon hides the Sun for a short time.

That is what we call an

eclipse.

When the Moon is right in front of the Sun, and hides the bright face, we can see the Sun's outer gas, which spreads out across the sky. We cannot see the gas except at the time of an eclipse, because the sky is too bright.

Eclipses like this do not happen often. The next one to be seen from England will be on August 11, 1999. Perhaps you will be lucky enough to see it!

AUG
11
1999

# How the Moon moves

The Sun can shine on only half of the Moon at once, so that one half of the Moon is bright and the other half is dark. This is why the Moon seems to change shape. When the Moon is almost between the Earth and the Sun, its dark side is turned towards us, and we cannot see the Moon at all; this is called new moon.

New moon

Quarter moon

As the Moon moves in its path, we begin to see a little of the bright side; then we see half of the bright side, and at full moon the whole of the bright side faces us. Because the Moon takes just over 27 days to go once round the Earth, we usually see one new moon and one full moon in every month.

Half moon

Full moon

# The face of the Moon

When you look at the Moon, you can see bright and dark patches. The dark patches are called seas, but they are not real seas; there is no water in them – and in fact there is no water anywhere on the Moon. There are high mountains, and there are many craters, which are really holes with walls round them.

The Moon's rocky surface

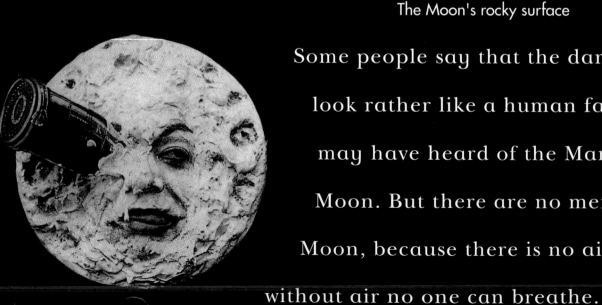

Some people say that the dark patches look rather like a human face – you may have heard of the Man in the Moon. But there are no men on the Moon, because there is no air, and without air no one can breathe.

The 'seas' on the Moon are low-lying plains.

A view of the Earth as it appears from the Moon.

# <u>*On the Moon*</u> If you could

go to the Moon, you would find that the sky

is black even in the daytime. Because there

is no air, there are no clouds and no wind;

of course it never rains on the Moon. The

days are much longer than ours. From the

Moon you would be able to see the Sun and the stars. You would

also see the Earth, which would look much bigger and brighter than

the Moon does to us. Sometimes the Earth would be new, sometimes

half and sometimes full, just as we see the Moon.

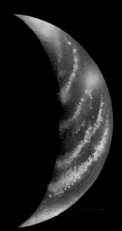
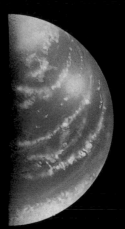

# Going to the Moon

There is no air between the Earth and the Moon, so that you cannot fly there in the same way as you can fly from London to America. Twelve men have been to the Moon, but they went there in rockets instead of aircraft. When you are on the Moon, you cannot go outside your rocket without putting on a space-suit, because there is no air for you to breathe. But before long we may have proper stations there, and it is possible that you will be able to visit it one day.

Neil Armstrong was the first man on the Moon.

The flag does not wave about, as it would do on Earth, because there is no air on the Moon.

# The planets

The Earth's Moon is not the only moon – just as the Earth is not the only planet. There are eight other planets, all moving round the Sun. Some of these planets have moons of their own.

The closest planet to the Sun is Mercury. Then comes Venus, our own Earth, and Mars, all of which are quite small. Further

Sun

Mercury

Venus

Earth

Mars

Asteroids

away than Mars there is a wide gap in which we find thousands of very small worlds which we call minor planets or asteroids.

Pluto

Neptune

Saturn

Jupiter

Uranus

Beyond come four very big planets, Jupiter, Saturn,

Uranus and Neptune, with one small planet, Pluto. If

you want to know the sizes of the planets, and the

times they take to go round the Sun, look at pages 92-

93 of this book.

Mars in the night sky

# Looking at the planets

Like the Moon, the planets have no light of their own. We can see them because they are being lit up

by the Sun, just as you can light up a football in a dark room by shining a lamp on it.

The stars are very like the Sun, and are very hot, but they seem much less bright than the Sun because they are further away. The planets look like stars, but they are really very different, and are much closer than any of the stars. They move slowly around in the sky, and this is how people first found out they are not at all like the stars.

# How the planets move

All the planets go round the Sun; the closer ones move much more quickly than those which are further away. The Earth takes one year (365 days) to go once round the Sun, but Mercury takes only 88 days, while Pluto takes 248 years. If you could live on Pluto, you would have to wait 248 years for your first birthday!

1 Mercury
2 Venus
3 Earth
4 Mars
5 Asteroids
6 Jupiter
7 Saturn
8 Uranus
9 Neptune
10 Pluto

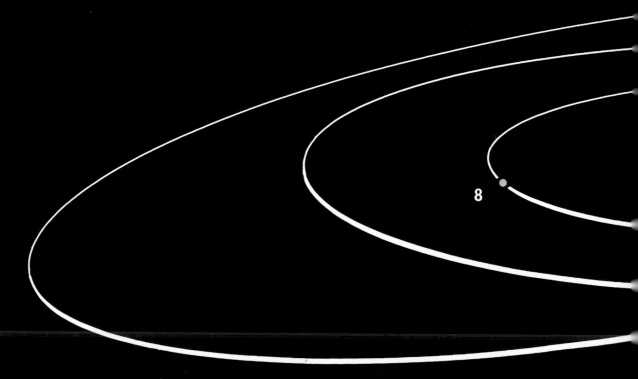

Venus, Mars, Jupiter and Saturn are so bright that you can find them easily. Mercury always keeps close to the Sun. You can just see Uranus but the two last planets, Neptune and Pluto, are so faint that you cannot see them at all unless you use a telescope.

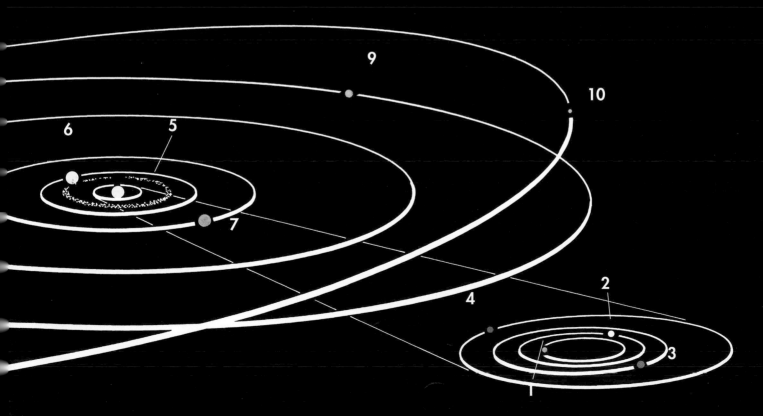

# Going to the planets

Although twelve men so far have been to the Moon, nobody has yet been to any of the planets. It would take a very long time to get there. But rockets have been sent past all the planets except Pluto, and have sent back pictures of them, so at least we know what they are like.

I am sure you have seen firework rockets. Rockets of this kind work in just the same way as the rockets which have been sent into space, but the space-rockets have very powerful rocket motors – otherwise they would not be able to go fast enough to escape from the Earth's gravity.

Saturn V rocket taking off

Mercury

# The hot planets

The first two planets, Mercury and Venus, are very hot. It is not easy to see Mercury, because it always stays so close to the Sun. It is small, and has no air, so nobody could live there.

The next planet, Venus, is nearly as big as the Earth. It can be very bright, and you can often see it in the west after sunset or in the east before the Sun rises. It has a very thick air, which we could not breathe, and it is so hot that any water there would boil away. It will be a long time before anyone can go to Venus for a visit.

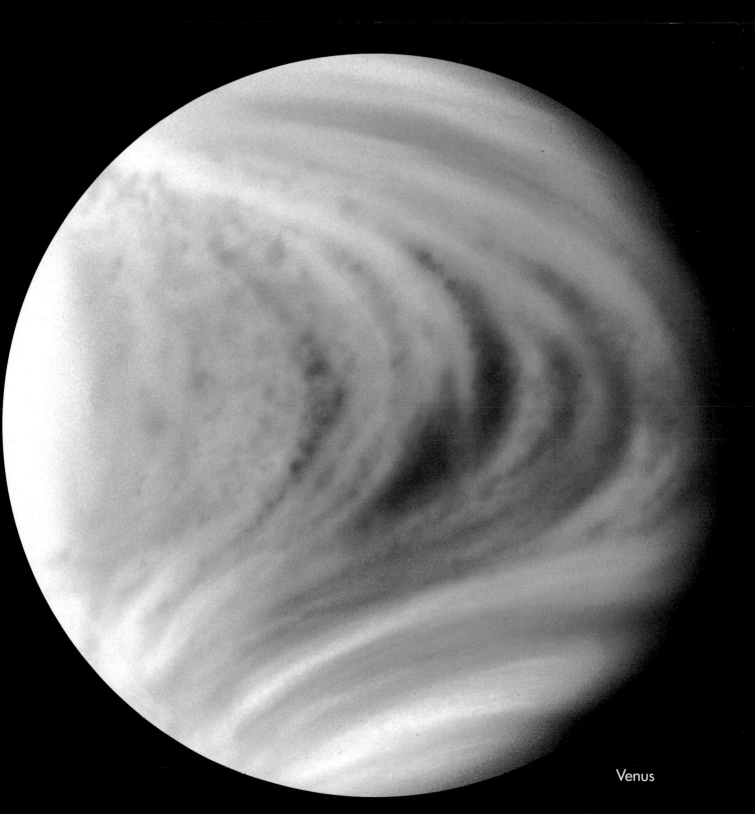

Venus

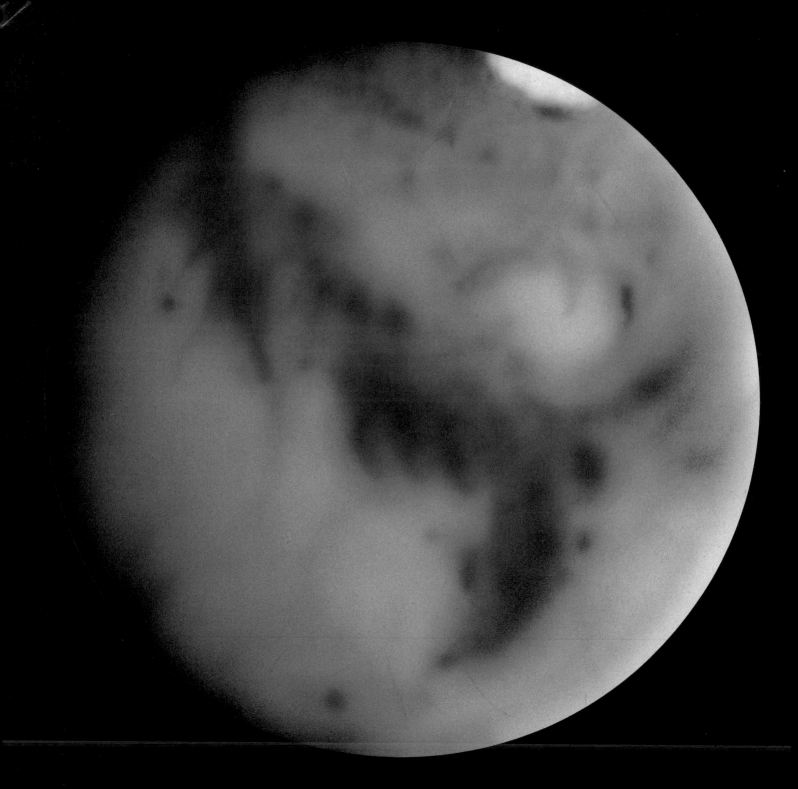

44

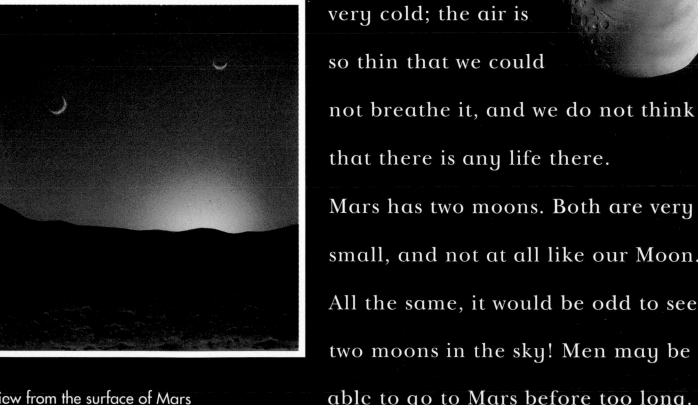

very cold; the air is so thin that we could not breathe it, and we do not think that there is any life there.

Mars has two moons. Both are very small, and not at all like our Moon. All the same, it would be odd to see two moons in the sky! Men may be able to go to Mars before too long.

View from the surface of Mars

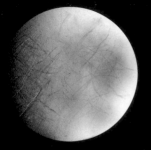

Europa

# *The biggest planet* Jupiter

is the biggest planet, and you can see it well for part of every year; it is much brighter than any of the stars. It takes nearly twelve years to go round the Sun, but it has a very short day, less than ten hours long.

Ganymede

Jupiter is not like Earth. Its surface is made up of gas, so we could never land a rocket there.

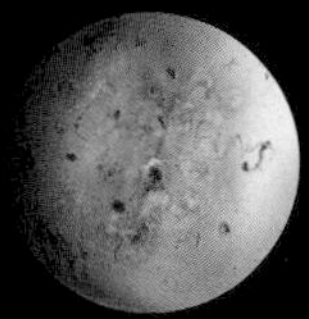

On Jupiter we can see lines which we call cloud belts. We can also see the Great Red Spot, which is a huge storm in Jupiter's gas.

Jupiter has 16 moons, and of these four are big; one of them, called Ganymede, is even bigger than the planet Mercury. You can see these four moons with any telescope.

Io

Callisto

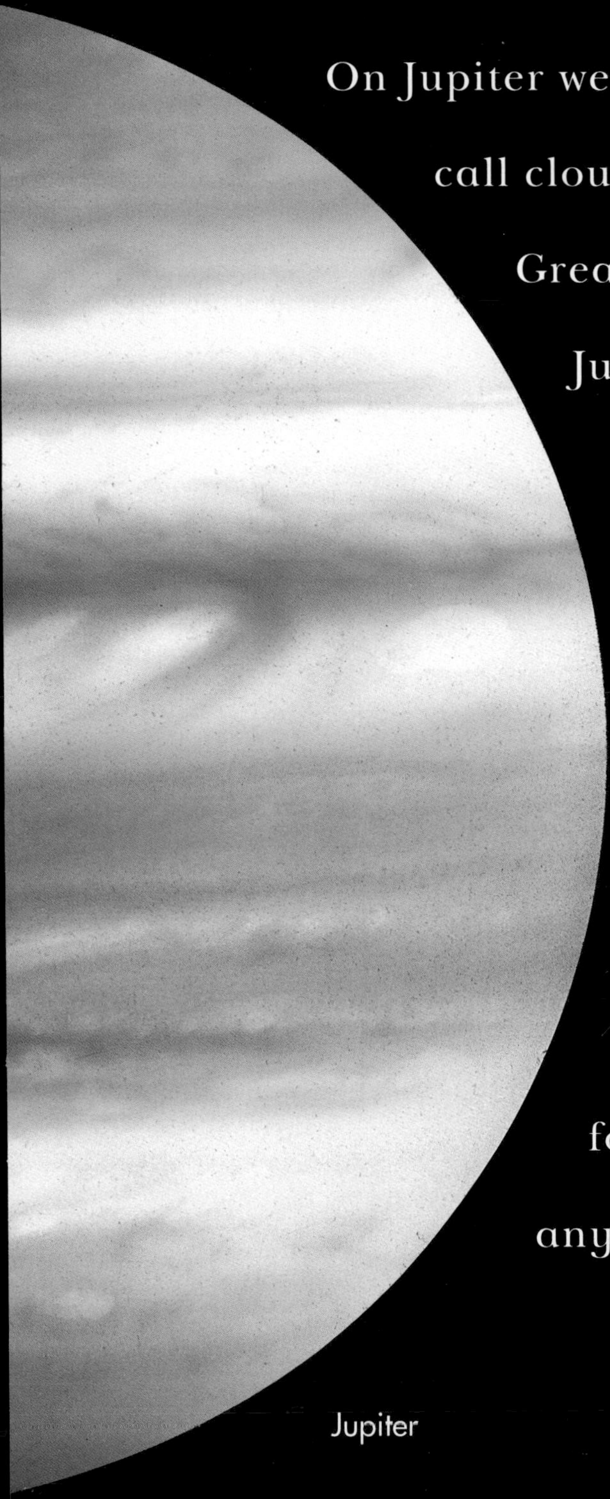

Jupiter

# The planet with the rings

The next planet is called Saturn. It is smaller than Jupiter, but much bigger than the Earth, and looks like a bright star in the sky.

Like Jupiter, Saturn has a surface made up of gas. It is very beautiful, because it has rings round it, though you cannot see them without a telescope. The rings are made up of little bits of ice moving around Saturn.

Saturn has 18 moons. One of these, named Titan, has a thick air, though it is so cold that we could not live there. If we could see through Titan's air, we might find seas on the surface. They would be very different from the seas we know on Earth.

Saturn's rings are made of pieces of ice.

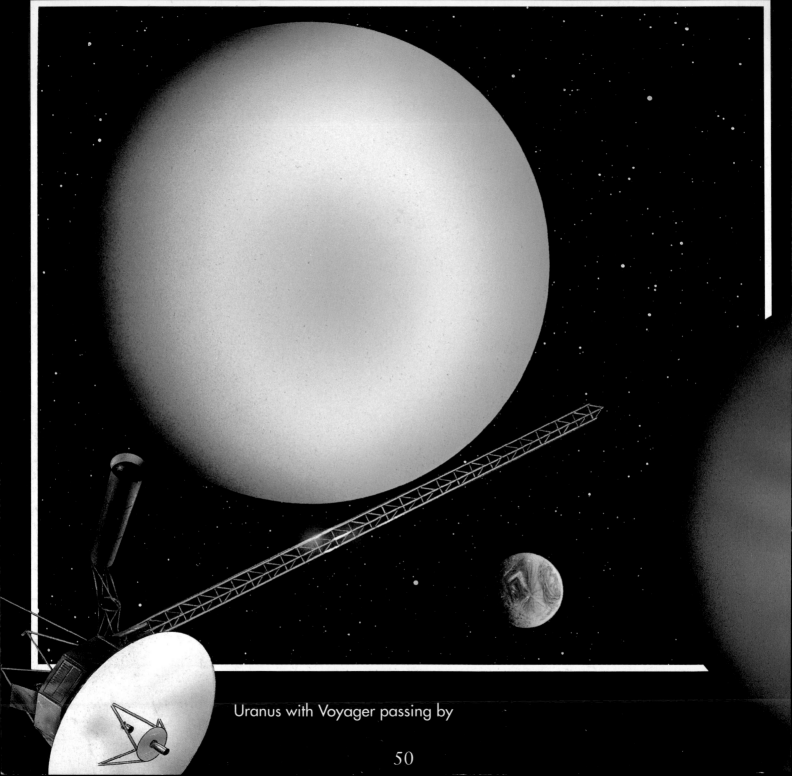

Uranus with Voyager passing by

# Very cold planets

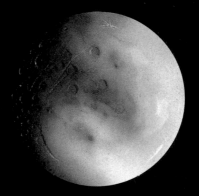

Pluto

The last three planets are so far away that they look faint. Uranus and Neptune are about half as big as Saturn, and both have moons; Uranus has 15 moons, Neptune, eight. Uranus is green, Neptune, blue. A space-ship called Voyager 2 passed by them both, so we have good pictures of them.

Pluto is smaller than our Moon, and no space-ship yet can reach it. It is so cold that air of the kind we know would freeze. If you could go to Pluto, the Sun would look only like a very bright star.

Now that you know what you are looking for, do go outdoors at night and find the closer planets for yourself!

Neptune

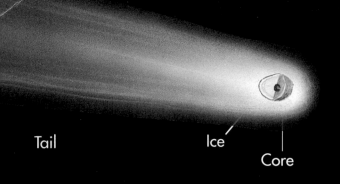

Tail                         Ice

Core

# *Comets*

Comets move round the Sun, but they are not like the Earth and the other planets. A comet is made up of a lump of ice, mixed with dust. As it moves through space, it leaves a trail of 'dust' behind it, and it is these pieces of 'dust' which we see as shooting-stars, or meteors, as they fall into the Earth's air.

A comet is a long way away, so that it does not move quickly across the sky in the same way as a meteor. You have to watch a comet for many hours before you can see that it is moving at all.

Shooting-stars are left behind by comets.

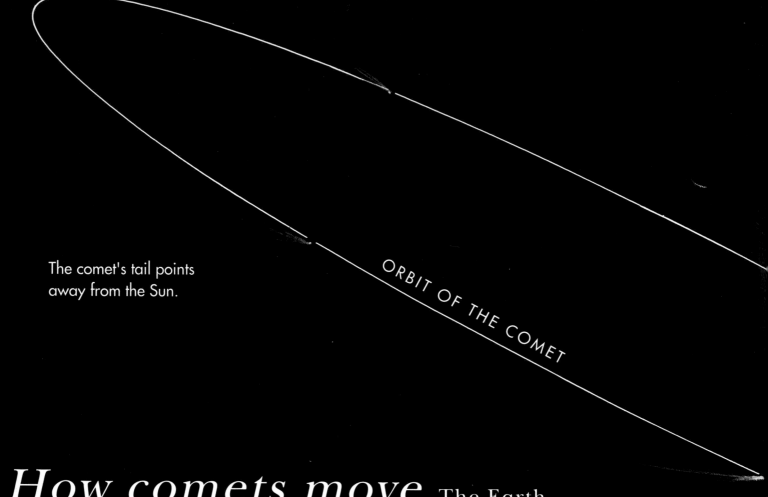

The comet's tail points away from the Sun.

ORBIT OF THE COMET

Earth

# How comets move The Earth

goes round the Sun in a path which is very like a

circle. A comet has a different sort of path. As you can see from the

picture, a comet may sometimes be much closer to the Sun than we

are, while at other times it will be much further away. Some comets

take only a few years to go once round the Sun, but others take a very long time indeed – many hundreds or even thousands of years.

A comet shines because it is being lit up by the Sun, so it is bright only when it is close to us. When it is a long way away, it becomes so faint that we cannot see it at all.

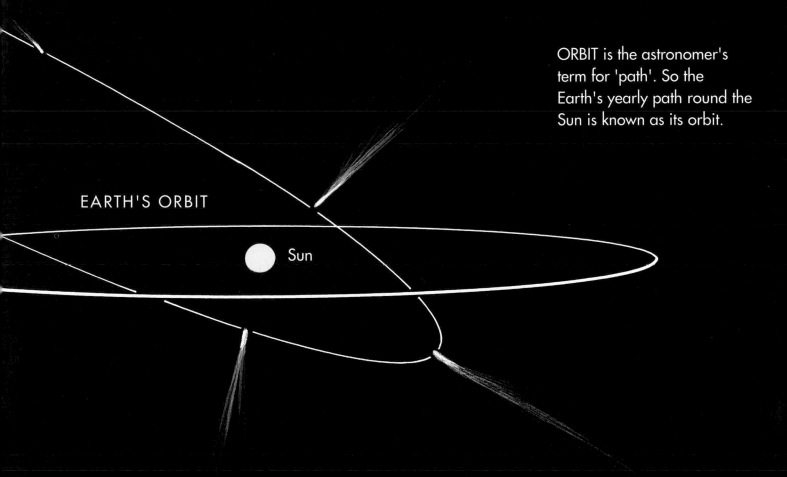

ORBIT is the astronomer's term for 'path'. So the Earth's yearly path round the Sun is known as its orbit.

EARTH'S ORBIT

Sun

Gases escaping from the nucleus form the comet's tail.

# The tails of comets

When a comet is a long way from the Sun it is very cold, and is nothing more than a frozen lump. When it moves closer to the Sun, and is warmed, the icy lump is surrounded by gas, making up what we call the comet's head.

A really big comet may also grow a long tail, stretching away from the Sun. There have even been some comets which have become so bright that they have cast shadows. No comets like this have been seen for many years now, and we do not know when the next one will appear.

# Halley's Comet

The best-known comet is called Halley's Comet, after an astronomer named Edmond Halley who first found out that it moves round the Sun. It appears every 76 years, and has been seen very often; it was in the sky just before the Battle of Hastings, in 1066, when William the Conqueror landed in England!

The Bayeux Tapestry, showing Halley's Comet, is 900 years old.

When it last came back, in 1986, five space-ships were sent to it, and one of these went right through the comet's head, sending back pictures of the icy lump in the middle.

Halley's Comet has now moved away from the Sun, and is too faint to be seen, but we know where it is. When it next comes back, in the year 2061, you may be lucky enough to see it for yourselves.

Halley's Comet passing the space probe Giotto

# Shooting-stars

Meteors come from comets. If you are looking into the sky on a dark night, when there are no clouds, you may sometimes see a streak of light which moves quickly across the night sky. This is what we call a meteor, or shooting-star. It is

not at all like a real star; it is only a tiny piece of 'dust' burning away in the Earth's upper air. Some meteors may become very bright, but they do not last for more than a few seconds before they disappear. They burn away long before they can fall to the ground.

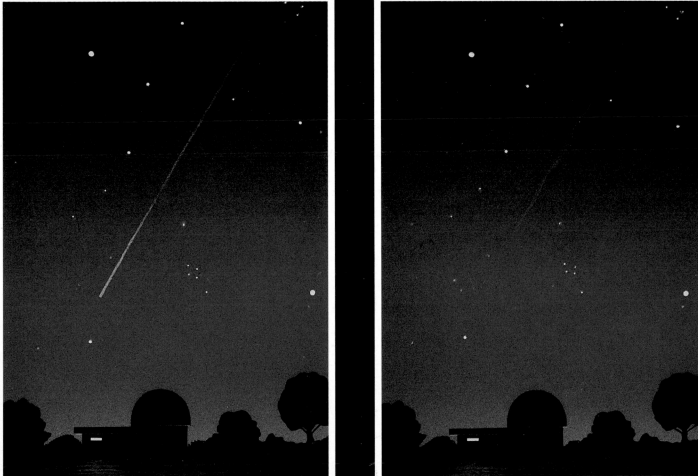

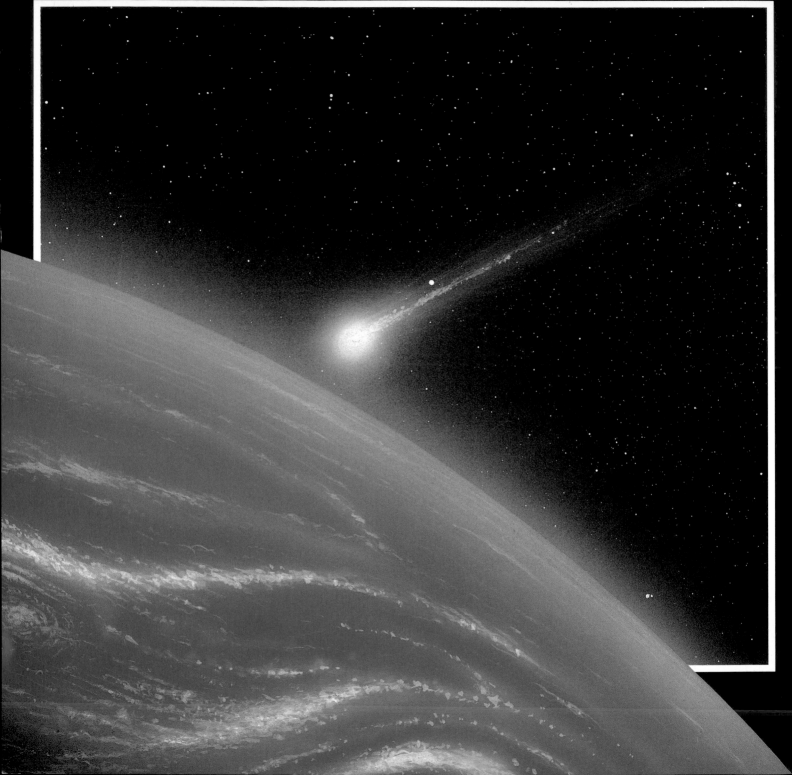

# *What makes a shooting-star?*

A meteor moves round the Sun in the same way as the Earth does. When it is in space, we cannot see it, because it is much too small. We see it only when it moves into the top of the Earth's air, and becomes hot because of what we call friction.

If you pump up a cycle tyre, you will find that the pump gets hot, because the air inside it is being squashed; this sets up friction, and this causes heat. A meteor moving into the upper air sets up so much heat by friction against the air that it catches fire, and burns away.

# *Showers of shooting-stars*

Meteors usually move round the Sun in bunches. When the Earth moves through one of these bunches, it collects a great many pieces of 'dust', and the result is a shower of shooting-stars.

This happens several times in every year, but the best time to see meteors is in the first part of August, when the Earth passes through a dense bunch. If you look up into a dark, clear sky for a few minutes at any time between the end of July and about August 17, you will probably be lucky enough to see several shooting-stars. Of course, you can see them at other times; meteors may appear at any moment.

# Stones from space

Sometimes the Earth meets a body which is big enough to drop right through the air without being burned away. It then lands on the Earth, and is called a meteorite.

Museums keep collections of meteorites; you can see them there. Most are made up of stone and iron. They do not come from comets, and are quite different from shooting-star meteors.

A really large meteorite may make a large hole or crater; one of these craters, in America, is over a kilometre wide. If the Earth were hit by a body of this kind there would be a great deal of damage, but luckily it is not

likely to happen; the crater in America is very old indeed. Nobody has ever been killed by a stone falling from space, so you can feel quite safe when you go outdoors at night to look for shooting-stars!

# Looking at the stars

When you look up into the sky at night-time, you will also see the stars. There are so many stars that you would find it hard to count them all. Some are very bright; others are dim. You cannot see the stars in the daytime, because the sky is too

bright, but they are always there. As soon as the Sun has set and the sky has become dark, the stars begin to show. They seem to twinkle, but this is only because the light from them has to come through the air above us. If the Earth had no air, the stars would not twinkle at all.

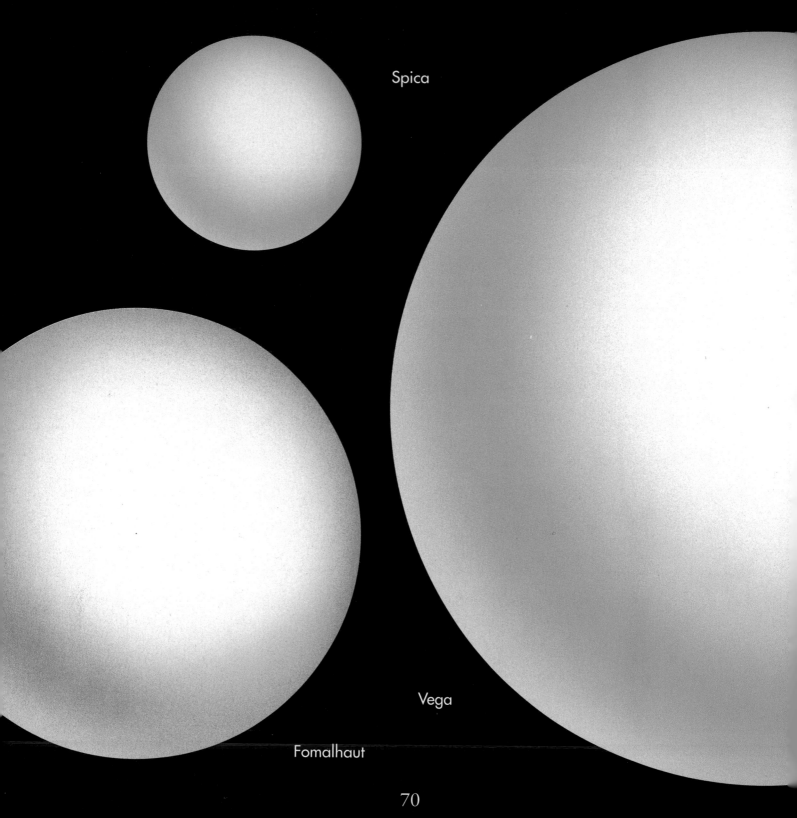

Spica

Vega

Fomalhaut

70

# What the stars are like

The stars look like tiny lamps in the sky, but they are really very big and hot. The Sun, which sends us all our light and heat, is only a star.

The Earth moves round the Sun, which looks much brighter than any of the other stars because it is much closer to us. The Sun is much bigger than the Earth, but we know that some of the stars are much bigger and hotter than the Sun. The stars look so small and faint only because they are such a long way away from us.

Our Sun

# _How the stars seem to move_

If you watch the night sky, you will see all the stars moving very slowly across the sky from east to west. But they are not really moving like this. They seem to do so because the Earth is turning round; this makes the sky seem to move, carrying all the stars with it.

The stars are not fixed to the sky. All of them are moving about, but they are so far away from us that they always seem to keep to the same groups.

The stars we see now look just the same as they did 2,000 years ago. Even their light takes many years to reach us, so that we do not see them as they are 'now'; we see them as they used to be

The night sky in this scene of long ago would look no different today.

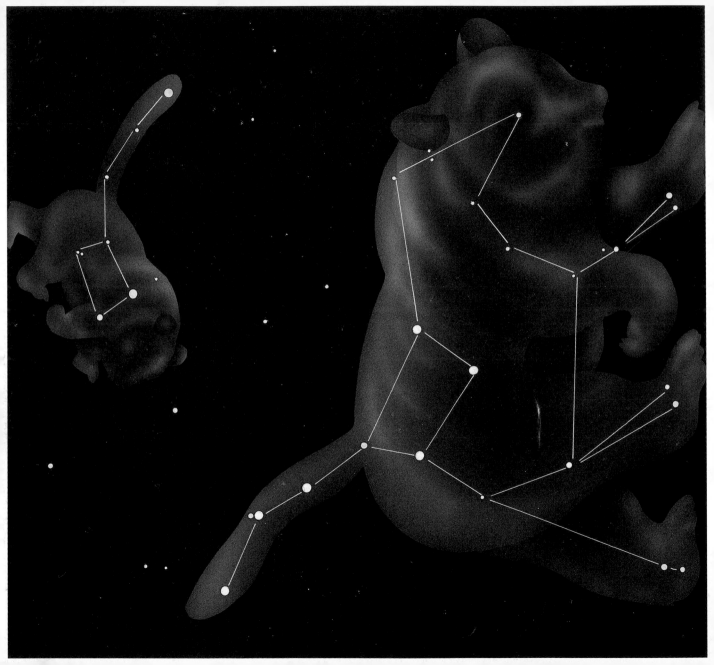

# The two bears in the sky

People who lived long ago gave names to the groups of stars, and made up stories about them. One of these stories was about two bears, who were pulled up by their tails and put into the sky. The Great Bear, sometimes called the Big Dipper, is shown by seven stars which make a shape which is very easy to find. The Little Bear is not so bright, but in it we find the north pole of the sky, close to the Pole Star. Once you have found the Pole Star you will always be able to find it again, because it does not seem to move at all.

In Australia or New Zealand, the Great Bear is very low in the sky, and you cannot see the Little Bear at all. But you can see new groups, such as the Southern Cross, which are never visible from Europe.

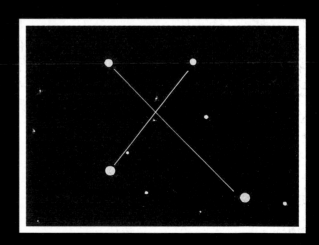

The Southern Cross

# The hunter and his dog

Another story is about a hunter who said that he could kill any animal he met. His name was Orion, and his stars are much brighter than those of the two Bears. You cannot always see Orion, because he is in the night sky for only part of the year. Orion is high up when it is winter in Britain, and summer in Australia. In Orion there are two very bright stars called Betelgeux and Rigel, and three stars in a line which make up the Hunter's Belt.

The Great Dog

Not far from Orion is the Great Dog, in which we find the brightest of all the night-time stars. Its name is Sirius, but most people just call it the Dog-Star. Further south, so that it can never be seen from Europe, is another very bright star, Canopus. In Australia you can see Canopus in the night sky for most of the year.

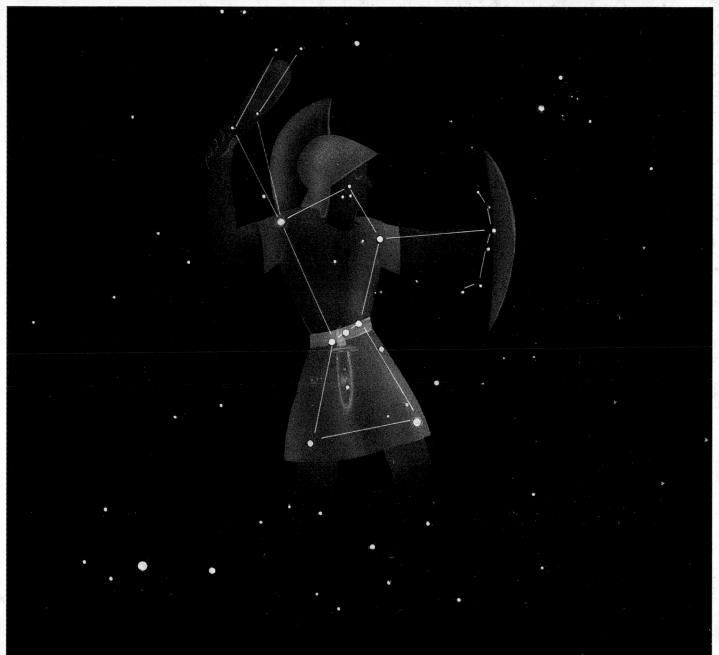

# The colours of the stars

White star (Sirius)

If you look at the stars, you will see that they are not all of the same colour. Our Sun is yellow; most of the night-time stars look white, but there are a few which are orange or red. This is because some of the stars are hotter than others.

White stars are hotter than yellow stars, while yellow stars are hotter than those which are orange or red. Most of the stars in Orion are white, but there is one which is red; this is the one named Betelgeux, but it is often called 'Beetle-juice'!

Yellow star
(Our Sun)

Red star
(Betelgeux)

Orange star
(Aldebaran)

# *How stars are born*

Here and there in the night sky we can see patches of dust and gas. There is a special name for them; they are called 'nebulae' (pronounced neb-you-lee), from an old word which means 'clouds'. Inside these clouds, new stars are being born. Long ago, our Sun was born in just the same way.

Some of the nebulae are easy to find. There is one in the star-group of Orion, the Hunter; you can see it near the three bright stars which make up the Hunter's Belt.

The Great Nebula in Orion, M42

# How stars die

The Sun, like all the other stars, cannot live forever. When it can no longer shine, it will become very dark and heavy, and then it will become cold and dark. Luckily this will not happen for a very long time, so there is no need to worry about the Sun going out. For thousands of millions of years yet the Sun will look just the same as it does now.

Some very big stars do not live for so long, and when they can no longer shine they blow up! Sometimes we can see a star doing this. For a few days or weeks it may be very bright, but before long it fades away.

But remember that the light from the stars takes years to reach us, so that when we watch a star blowing up we are seeing something which really happened a long time ago.

The Milky Way in the night sky

# The Milky Way

If you live away from a town, and there are no lights near you, you will be able to see the Milky Way. This looks like a band of light crossing the night sky. It is made up of stars which look as if they are very close together.

This is not really true. The system of stars in which we live is shaped rather like two fried eggs put together back to back. When we look along the thick part of the system, we can see many stars almost one behind the other, and it is this which makes up the Milky Way.

Side view of our Galaxy

We have a special name for the system of stars in which we live; we call it the Galaxy. In it there are at least a hundred thousand million stars.

# *Other galaxies*

Our Milky Way Galaxy is not the only one. There are many others, most of them so far away that their light takes millions of years to reach us. We also know that except for a few of the closer galaxies, all of them are moving away from us, so that the whole universe is spreading out. Many of the galaxies are what we call 'spirals', as shown in the picture; in fact our own Galaxy is a spiral, and the Sun, together with the Earth, lies near the edge of one of the spiral arms.

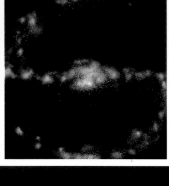

S-shaped galaxy

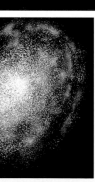

Elliptical galaxy

Top view of our Galaxy as it would be seen from a spacecraft a million light years away. The arrow points to our Earth.

# Getting to know the stars

When you first look up into a sky which seems to be full of stars, you may think that you will never be able to tell one from another. But because the stars are so far away, the groups do not change, and this makes it easy to learn your way around.

A group of stars is called a 'constellation', but the stars in any constellation are not really close to each other; they are at very different distances from us, so that one star in a constellation may be a long way 'behind' another.

Soon you will recognise different constellations. You will be able to find the Bears, Orion the Hunter, and all the others visible from your part of the Earth; you will be able to see the red and orange stars, the gas-clouds and much more. If you take a star-map and go out at night, you will quickly find that you are making friends with all the stars.

The Hubble space telescope can see a very long way into space.

# <u>*Other Earths?*</u> Although our

star, the Sun, has eight other planets besides

the Earth moving around it, we could not live

on any of them. Some are too hot; others are too

cold, and they do not have the right sort of air for us to breathe.

But it may well be that other stars have planets of their

own, with life on them.

If this is true – and we cannot be sure! – then there

may be people like ourselves. We cannot send space-

ships to planets of other stars, because they are too far away, but

one day we may be able to find out that we are not

alone in space. Whether this happens or not, we

may be sure that in the next few years we are

going to discover many new and exciting facts

about space and our Universe.

Here are some facts about the planets

which you may like to know.

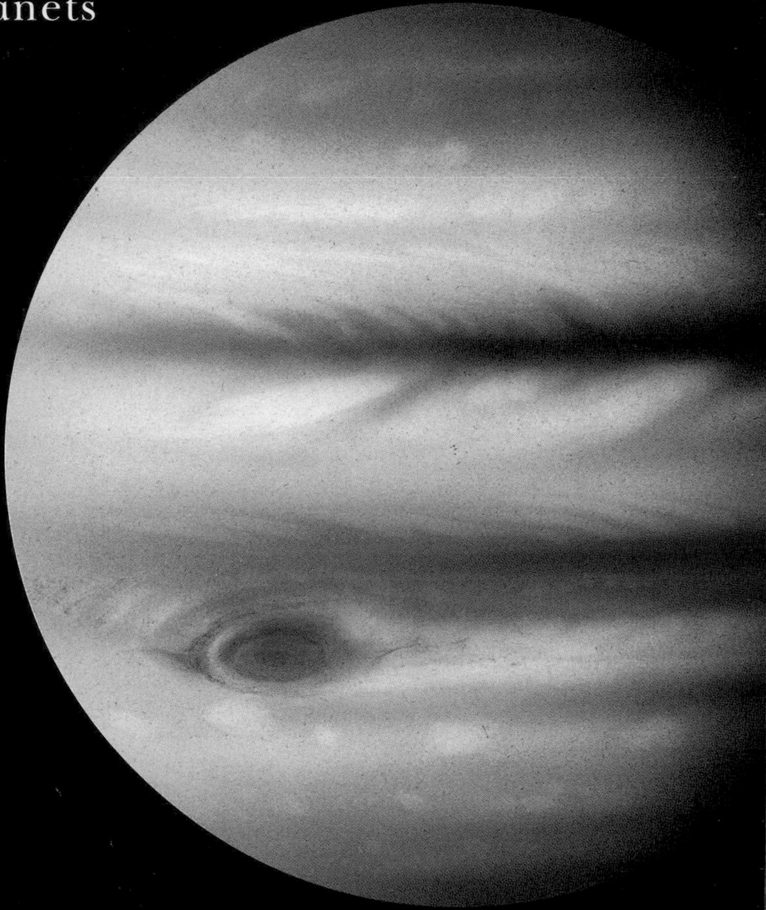

**MERCURY**
58
88 days
58 days
4,878
0

**VENUS**
108
225 days
243 days
12,104
0

**EARTH**
150
365¼ days
24 hours
12,756
1

**MARS**
228
687 days
24½ hours
6,794
2

**JUPITER**
778
11¾ years
9¾ hours
142,800
16

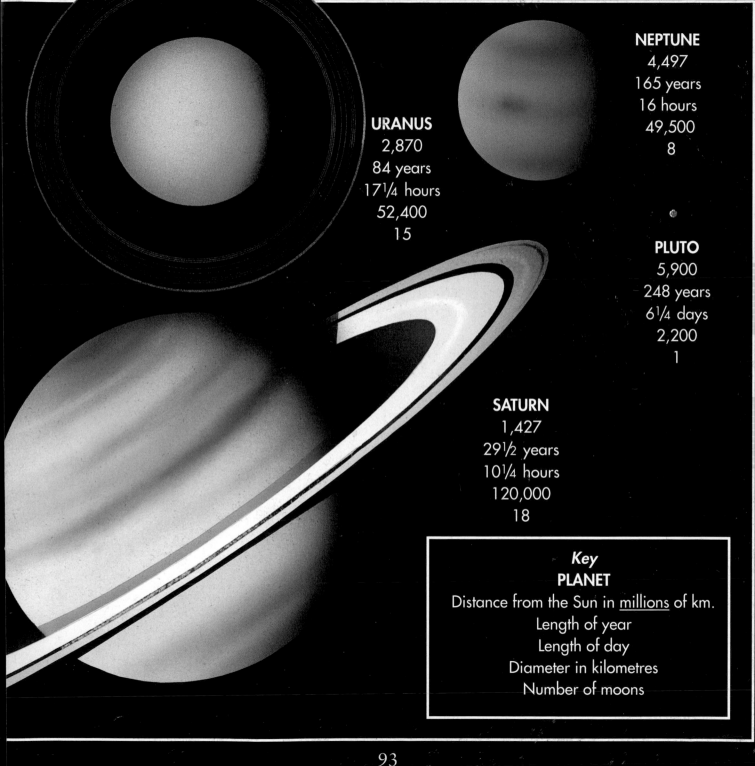

**URANUS**
2,870
84 years
17¼ hours
52,400
15

**NEPTUNE**
4,497
165 years
16 hours
49,500
8

**PLUTO**
5,900
248 years
6¼ days
2,200
1

**SATURN**
1,427
29½ years
10¼ hours
120,000
18

***Key***
**PLANET**
Distance from the Sun in <u>millions</u> of km.
Length of year
Length of day
Diameter in kilometres
Number of moons

# Index